OLD BARNS – NEW HOMES

A Showcase of
Architectural Conversions

Old Barns – New Homes

A Showcase of Architectural Conversions

E. Ashley Rooney

With Foreword by
Peter Gerhard Stampfl, AIA, NCARB

Schiffer Publishing Ltd

4880 Lower Valley Road, Atglen, PA 19310 USA

Front cover: *Top:* Courtesy of Nick Wheeler, Photography
Left to right: Courtesy of Thomas G. Anglim, AIA, CCM; Courtesy of D. Peter Lund; Courtesy of D. Peter Lund

Back cover: Courtesy of Nick Wheeler, Photography

Spine: Courtesy of George Holback

Frontispiece: Courtesy of George Holback

Title page: Courtesy of Thomas G. Anglim, AIA, CCM

Copyright © 2003 Tim Wilkes 585.423.1966.

Library of Congress Cataloging-in-Publication Data

Rooney, E. Ashley.
    Old barns, new homes : a showcase of architectural conversions / by E. Ashley Rooney.
        p. cm.
    ISBN 0-7643-2132-3
    1. Barns—United States. 2. Barns—Remodeling for other use—United States. 3. Architecture, Domestic—United States. I. Title.

NA8230.R66 2005
728'.922'0286—dc22

2004019900

Designed by Mark David Bowyer
Type set in Script12 BT/Humanist521 BT

ISBN: 0-7643-2132-3
Printed in China

Published by Schiffer Publishing Ltd.
4880 Lower Valley Road
Atglen, PA 19310
Phone: (610) 593-1777; Fax: (610) 593-2002
E-mail: Info@schifferbooks.com

For the largest selection of fine reference books on this and related subjects, please visit our web site at
www.schifferbooks.com
We are always looking for people to write books on new and related subjects. If you have an idea for a book please contact us at the above address.

This book may be purchased from the publisher.
Include $3.95 for shipping.
Please try your bookstore first.
You may write for a free catalog.

In Europe, Schiffer books are distributed by
Bushwood Books
6 Marksbury Ave.
Kew Gardens
Surrey TW9 4JF England
Phone: 44 (0) 20 8392-8585; Fax: 44 (0) 20 8392-9876
E-mail: info@bushwoodbooks.co.uk
Free postage in the U.K., Europe; air mail at cost.

CONTENTS

Preface
6

Foreword
Uniquely American –
Barn to Residence Conversions
9

Chapter One
The Barn of the Past
15

Chapter Two
Barn Decoration
25

Chapter Three
The Barn of Today
35

Chapter Four
Residential Conversions
47

Courtesy of Ozzie (Rvoni Photo).

Chapter Five
Commercial and Other Conversions
131

Chapter Six
A Barn from Scratch
163

Chapter Seven
Wadsworth Village
169

Appendix
Architects, Builders,
and Other Lovers of American Barns
174

Bibliography
176

Project Index
176

THE BARN OF THE PAST

Generally, we think of American barns as large, rectangular structures built from wood with few, if any, windows and a huge double door. They are big, and they are red.

The early colonists knew the importance of barns. The New England climate dictated that their animals had to have appropriate shelter in the winter and that their feed be stored in a sound, sturdy structure.

Although they built their houses slowly, they laid their barns out on the ground and raised them several days later with the help of the neighbors and friends. From the very beginning, the American barn was big.

Built on a European model, the early barns had steeply slanted thatched roofs, and siding was horizontal. Doors had wooden hinges; beams were hand-hewn, and wooden pins acted as nails.

Barns are part of our history. They were the beginning of our nation, the start of our prosperity. *Courtesy of D. Peter Lund.*

Soon, American farmers began to design barns that were more appropriate to the rigorous New England climate. Thatch gave way to clapboard and bark shingles. Barns were built higher, and the roof became less slanted.

Immigrants brought different barn designs and construction techniques from the old country. They built barns to fit the region, the climate, the crops, and their ethnic background.

The Pennsylvania barn was often made of stone and brick and nestled against a hillside. In Virginia, barns were used for drying tobacco. Flimsy structures, they had hinged sideboards for ventilation. In New England, barns connected to the houses so the farmer could reach his livestock without venturing out into the snowstorms. In the Southwest, barns were larger in size and detached. They stored hay for range herds.

A red barn is synonymous with America. *Courtesy of Whitney Gay.*

The Basic Multi-Purpose Barn

The first barns were not much more than crude log and post structures. But as an area became settled, the barns took shape.

The early New England barns housed livestock, the cows, horses, and pigs, on the bottom floor. The floor above them stored grain and fodder on both sides of a central open area. This area in the middle was used for threshing grain, a practice that goes back to ancient Egypt. Tucked in crannies here and there were farm implements and feed grains.

Until approximately 1830, settlers in New England based the construction of their barns on a standard English design: It was 30 feet by 40 feet with a simple gable roof. Rough sawn boards installed vertically sheathed the walls. As the lumber was usually green when nailed, the boards would shrink upon drying, resulting in large gaps between boards. By the 1840s, battens to cover these gaps were used. The 1860s saw the use of horizontal spruce or cedar clapboards.

Enormous timbers framed the barn. Usually made of oak, a barn was pegged together in a series of bents or H frames. The main frames were perpendicular to the roof ridge and, depending on the size of the barn, there were three or more of them. The uprights rose from floor to roof. The crosspieces were set high above the floor so loaded farm carts could pass below.

Viewed from front or back, the barn was divided into three wide aisles called bays. When seen from the sides, the barn was divided into transverse bays, the number depending on the number of bents.

Barns could have several levels above the main floor. These did not necessarily have a solid floor. Instead, planks were often thrown across the transverse beams. The hay was stored in these upper levels. Large, long, well-spaced rafters that met at the ridge made up the barn roof. The hayloft door nestled under the peak of the roof.

The wagon door was generally centered in the front wall. Often, there was a similar doorway in the back wall so a wagon could pass straight through the barn instead of backing out. Any windows were placed haphazardly. Natural lighting was not considered a priority.

Since damp hay can burst spontaneously into flame, good ventilation was essential. Older barns were often ventilated by pigeon holes scattered about the upper sidewalls. To improve ventilation, farmers often added cupolas.

A bank barn in Pennsylvania.
Courtesy of D. Peter Lund.

The farmer tried to place his barn centrally so that extensive traveling wasn't required. If the farmer was successful, he might add other farm buildings, such as a chicken coop or pigpen, near the barn.

Before the 1850s, most barns had at least one pair of hinged doors or a single sliding door on double metal strips. Later, the single sliding door on rollers became common. During the nineteenth century, gable entry barns that often had a long transom window set above the wagon doors to provide light became popular. This became known as the New England barn.

Then there are the stables or horse barns and the carriage houses. Stables are generally long, narrow, one-story buildings with windows and a door into each stall. Carriage houses generally have some of the architectural features of the main residence.

The majesty of timbers stands out in old barns. *Courtesy of D. Peter Lund.*

Note the transom above the wagon doors on this barn. *Courtesy of D. Peter Lund.*

Regional Differences

When people think of the classic New England barn, they often think of the barn that is attached to the house through a series of small subsidiary buildings such as a woodshed, tool house, or milk house. The typical arrangement is the big house, little house, back house, and barn.

This rambling design is seen in Maine, Massachusetts, New Hampshire, and Vermont – states where the snow can accumulate several feet deep and the winter wind is fierce. Known as continuous architecture, this structure can dart off at an angle or run in a straight line. The farmer can walk from house to barn and be sheltered from the winter's storms.

Built between 1630 and 1825 in the New York area, New World Dutch barns differ from other historic barns in their distinctive shape, arrangement of interior space, and H-shaped structural frames. These provide a rigid core supporting the external roofing and walls. Generally, their width is larger than their length. They have a broad steep roof rising from low sidewalls. Large wagon doors, often accompanied by a smaller, human-size door, are centered under the gable. Holes near the roofline allow the barn swallows to flit in and out.

The interior includes a broad center aisle with a plank floor designed to accommodate unloading wagons and to provide space for grain threshing. Flanking side aisles provided storage and housing for livestock.

As pioneers moved west, and settlers arrived from Germany, Scandinavia, Holland, and other countries, new barn designs appeared. Over time, most farmers and builders adapted their barns to the climate, geography, local building materials, and changes in agricultural practice.

The typical bank barn or the Pennsylvania Dutch barn begins as a sheltered hillside structure with one side of the basement wall up against the hill. The barn faces south, and the barnyard is on the sunny side so the livestock could be led out from the lower floor, which was dug out of the hillside. Since the floor opened only to the south and was protected from the northerly winds by the hill, the animals were sheltered from the cold. The driveway on the north side leading up the rise to the main threshing floor on the second story is a characteristic feature of the building.

Note the small buildings between the house and the barn. This Massachusetts residence has been restored. *Courtesy of D. Peter Lund.*

The early German and Swiss settlers who built these barns were familiar with the fore bay barns of Switzerland. In most bank barns, the main or upper part overhung the lower part on the south side by as much as 10 feet. This fore bay or overshoot varies widely according to local tradition and available materials.

Farmers threw the hay down the stairway or into the straw room, where it was fed to the livestock. The threshing areas and granaries were overhead on the barn floor.

These barns are noteworthy for their extensive stonework. The thick, 18- to 30-inch walls are distinguished by a series of loopholes or gable windows providing light and ventilation.

Crib barns are found in the South and Southwest. Not as tall as their northern brothers, their long wide roofs provide storage space for hay and feed. In the earliest ones, farmers built the middle section from closely placed horizontal logs. In the wings, they spaced the logs or planks as in a corncrib. Today, boards or metal sheets are used.

The first Western barns, also known as the prairie barn, were cattle shelters made of poles with roofs of straw. The long, wide roof furnishes shelter from storms and provides storage for hay and feed.

Round barns, including many-sided ones, can be found around the country. The largest concentrations of this style of barn are found in Indiana, Illinois, and Wisconsin. Generally located on wealthy farms, they became popular in the late 1800s.

George Washington's 16-sided barn built in 1793 is the earliest recorded barn of this type. The Shaker Barn in Hancock, Massachusetts, built in 1825 is probably the most famous. It was 90 feet in diameter with 30-inch stone walls. After it burned down, the Shakers built another on the same site in 1865.

Initially, octagonal or sixteen-sided barns were the first to catch on. By the early 1890s, round barns came into fashion. Some believe that barns were built round to prevent "the devil from hiding in the corners."

Their design, however, is based on the theory that there is more floor space and less wall space in a circle or polygon than in a rectangle. They resist strong winds better than traditional barns because strong gusts are directed around the structure rather than directly at the walls.

This house and attached barn are in the process of being restored. The barn will become an elegant family room.
Courtesy of Paul Doherty.

The New World Dutch barn, as it has come to be known, is one of the remaining vestiges of the pre-industrial agricultural heritage of eastern New York and New Jersey. Built in large numbers before 1850, these barns served as all-purpose working farm buildings in a region dominated by grain farming. *Courtesy of Whitney Gay.*

By combining one- and two-story sections in the same structure, Pennsylvania farmers utilized the gently rolling terrain, nestling their structures into a hillside. This technique also helped to moderate the temperature inside these early barns. This bank barn has openings for additional ventilation. *Courtesy of Whitney Gay.*

Most round barns are built with a silo in the center. The round shape facilitates feeding and milking cows. The silo is loaded from the top, and the farmer forks the silage out at the bottom and feeds it directly to the encircling cows.

Above: A round barn in Iowa. *Courtesy of Maxheim Photography.*

Right: In 1919, Peter Tonsfeldt built this round barn in Lemars, Iowa, to show his purebred livestock and prized polled Hereford bull named "Ito's Perfection." Once the agricultural prices collapsed after the war, Tonsfeldt lost his farm. Ultimately, the barn was moved to the Plymouth County Fairgrounds in Lemars, Iowa. *Courtesy of Maxheim Photography.*

Chapter Two

BARN DECORATION

Generally, the American farmer did not construct his barn as a showplace. He built it from necessity. Consequently, barns are generally simple, sturdy, utilitarian structures. Decorative treatments are rare. When he had some money, the American farmer might paint his barn, but he did little to decorate it.

There are some things, however.

Cupola

A cupola is a small, domed structure made of wood. In the days before roof and ridge vents, a cupola was the most effective way to ventilate a stable, barn, or even a house. Most had louvered side openings to evacuate the accumulating heat. Cupolas were also a way that the farmer could decorate his barn and exercise his sense of creativity.

Today, people put cupolas and weather vanes on their barns and garages as well as their homes, but most are purely decorative and many are too small for the structure that supports them.

Cupolas come in many shapes and styles. *Courtesy of D. Peter Lund and Whitney Gay.*

Weather Vane

A weather vane pointing in the wind can tell the farmer whether a northerly wind is bringing frost or a southerly wind says spring is on its way. Early American farmers were dependent upon these devices to forecast changes in the weather.

Originally, farmers used weather vanes for telling the direction of the wind. *Courtesy of D. Peter Lund.*

The first weather vanes were sensitive, wooden instruments. *Courtesy of D. Peter Lund.*

Today they are usually just decorative.
Courtesy of D. Peter Lund.

A barn without a weather vane looks naked.
Courtesy of D. Peter Lund.

Paint

Most farmers had little time to worry about architectural ornament or painted decoration. Toward the end of the eighteenth century, farmers became more interested in painting their barns, especially if they were feeling rich.

Painted barns became even more common by the late nineteenth century. New England farmers produced a strong, plastic-like paint from skim milk, red iron oxide, and lime. These mundane ingredients give the American barn its noteworthy red paint. Red paint is durable, easily made, and absorbs the heat of the sun, thus adding to the warmth of the barn. Later, farmers switched from milk to linseed oil to get better penetration.

This red barn is a classic bit of Americana. *Courtesy of D. Peter Lund.*

Hex Signs

Folklore tells us that local Pennsylvania German farmers put colorful symbols called "hex signs" on their barns to keep the evil spirits away or to bring good luck. These "folk art" designs of rosettes, stars, circles, and the "Tree of Life" with their connection to the sun, nature, and the celestial, can be seen on everything from tombstones and birth certificates, to furniture and plates.

A more common interpretation of the hex sign is as an indicator of "ethnic symbolism." The earliest documented hex signs on barns date back to the later half of the nineteenth century, perhaps because barns weren't generally painted much before 1830. Around 1940, painters started making hex signs that could be purchased and mounted on barns and other buildings. These colorful decorations began to appear on tourist literature and on locally made products, becoming an easy way to "identify" the product as coming from the Pennsylvania Dutch region.

Hex signs can be found on barns and are sold to tourists. *Courtesy of D. Peter Lund.*

Other Decorative Treatments

Some farmers became very creative in personalizing their barns.

This barn, located in Pennsylvania, has become known as the "champagne barn" because of the shape of the vents in its stone walls. *Courtesy of Whitney Gay.*

These vents create a vertical accent against the stonewalls of this barn. *Courtesy of Whitney Gay.*

CHEW
MAIL POUCH TOBACCO
TREAT YOURSELF TO THE BEST

This Pennsylvania barn is called the Mail Pouch barn for obvious reasons. *Courtesy of Whitney Gay.*

This farmer liked a checkered silo. *Courtesy of Whitney Gay.*

Chapter Three

The Barn of Today

Light studded walls and trussed roofs replaced the heavy, pegged post and beam framing on barns. *Courtesy of D. Peter Lund.*

Top: Sliding doors, manure trolleys, silos, cupolas, and lightning rods became common, and individual differences began to wane. *Courtesy of Whitney Gay.*

Bottom: By the end of the nineteenth century, new laborsaving devices and improved cultivation and husbandry methods made farming more efficient. *Courtesy of D. Peter Lund.*

Agricultural monoliths began to replace the family farm. *Courtesy of D. Peter Lund.*

Barns became prefabricated behemoths. Ultimately, the family farm came close to vanishing. *Courtesy of Whitney Gay.*

RESIDENTIAL CONVERSIONS

Although old barns are rapidly disappearing, many people still appreciate their simplicity, symmetry, and integrity. To some of us, they represent an old-fashioned simplicity in this dot.com world where even the microwave takes too long. Others recognize that their vast space and great exposed timbers help make them striking and comfortable homes. Still others find the intrinsic character of these old barns brings an integrity and charm rarely seen in new construction.

The tremendous flexible space offered by barns can give rise to many creative solutions. Home and business owners are discovering that barns offer grand spaces, striking construction, and the imaginative play of sunlight and shadow. In recent years, the conversion of barns into residences, offices, retail establishments, nonprofit centers and the like has become increasingly popular among those seeking to preserve our heritage.

Many creative architects and owners have made barns useful through renovation and adaptive commercial re-use. Some examples are provided in the following pages.

Abandoned Dairy Barn Conversion

Thomas Anglim, AIA, CCM, converted a 1930s vintage dairy barn in Great Falls, Virginia, to a beautiful residence. Although the barn was abandoned, it remained structurally sound. The client requested that the firm save each of the three separate structures: main barn, silo, and milk room.

Today, the silo contains a home office with a loft library above. The main barn houses a great room, dining room, and kitchen on the upper level, with bedrooms and a family room on the lower level. The milk room became a guestroom and cabana for the pool.

South façade shows the milk room to the right, main barn in the center, and silo on the left. *Courtesy of Thomas G. Anglim, AIA, CCM.*

This close up of the west façade is taken from the new entrance drive.
Courtesy of Thomas G. Anglim, AIA, CCM.

The main entrance to the home connects the silo to the main barn on two levels. *Courtesy of Thomas G. Anglim, AIA, CCM.*

North and east façade show the main barn and the milk room.

Courtesy of Thomas G. Anglim, AIA, CCM.

This image depicts the silo connection.
Courtesy of Thomas G. Anglim, AIA, CCM.

Six new dormers were added to increase interior light in the main barn's upper level.
Courtesy of Thomas G. Anglim, AIA, CCM.

The image is of the west façade taken from the entrance drive. *Courtesy of Thomas G. Anglim, AIA, CCM.*

There's a grand feeling of air and light here, partially resulting from the addition of the dormers. *Courtesy of Thomas G. Anglim, AIA, CCM.*

The great room has a stone fireplace. *Courtesy of Thomas G. Anglim, AIA, CCM.*

The Residence at Corbetts Glen

The Rochester Chapter/AIA recognized the residence at Corbetts Glen, designed by L. William Chapin, II, FAIA, for design excellence. Chapin employed interior wall angles to achieve spatial drama and clarity within the barn while optimizing the best vistas of the site. The cupola at the center of the home was rotated 45 degrees off axis to reinforce the angles of the rest of the design.

William Chapin based his barn conversion design on his desire to take advantage of views that occur at 45-degree angles to the long axis of the barn. In response, diagonal axes were superimposed on the rectangular plan of the barn. *Courtesy of L. William Chapin, II, FAIA-Architect.*

After the sagging barn frame was jacked up to plumb, it was let down on two newly constructed interior bearing walls. *Courtesy of L. William Chapin, II, FAIA-Architect.*

In the interest of design continuity and optimum use of the space, all the major architectural elements such as the stair tower, cupola, chimneys, and bay windows conform to the 45-degree angles of the floor plan. The spaces on all three levels are organized around the interior stair tower.

Courtesy of L. William Chapin, II, FAIA-Architect.

The cupola at the top of the tower brings light
into the core of the house. *Courtesy of L. William Chapin, II.*
FAIA-Architect.

The once-dark barn is now light-filled in all areas, including the kitchen and the bedrooms.

Courtesy of L. William Chapin, II, FAIA-Architect.

Courtesy of L. William Chapin, II, FAIA-Architect.

The old barn stands proudly in its new guise. *All images this page courtesy of L. William Chapin, II, FAIA-Architect.*

Details. All images this page courtesy of D. Peter Lund.

The conversion has turned it into a charming abode with plenty of space for family and friends. *Courtesy of D. Peter Lund.*

Today, the third story cupola offers dramatic views of Cape Cod Bay when the leaves have disappeared. It is believed to have been designated as a landmark on old maritime charts.

Courtesy of D. Peter Lund.

Converted Horse Barn

Converted in 1965, this barn is of single board construction and unheated, except for a fireplace.

Once an old horse barn, this structure now makes a great vacation home. It looks out on a meadow.

The two-storied room is well lit.

The great room is spacious,
and the fireplace keeps it
warm on chilly mornings.

65

There is light throughout the house.

Yet outside there are many trees.

The kitchen is spacious with a great deal of storage.

The owners made the south side the main entrance and constructed a garage this past year.

The house and grounds keep growing and changing.

The gazebo was built about twenty years ago. They landscaped the south side, and the bedroom has its own brick patio and entrance. This house has been a continuing and exciting renovation project.

The original barn doors remain on rollers and lead into the bullpen, now used as a poolroom. Open gratings, a horse stall wall, and an oak newel post, all remnants from the barn's past, surround the bullpen.

Restored hard yellow pine beams offset the living room's contemporary furnishings. It has a see-through fireplace.
Four glass sliding doors provide passive solar heat in the living room. Huge barn doors outside the sliders can be pulled to provide privacy.

Left: Three horses once fed in the space now used as a kitchen. Its distinctive slat ceiling was crafted from 1 by 4 inch fir. Quarry tile flooring provides color contrast to the snow-white walls and cabinets. Racek left the three feeding doors intact. They open into the 2,300 square foot family room.

Below: Skylights and natural beams cap the vaulted ceiling in the master bedroom. The sitting room fireplace invites relaxation.

What a grand place to grow up.

10-12 Degree Tilt

This barn was originally part of an estate. All the other land was sold for single-family homes, and the barn was left empty for several years. Previously, it had been used as a horse stable and a storage area.

When Gene Racek of E.R. Racek Associates purchased this barn, it was leaning 10 to 12 degrees and had to be rebuilt from the ground up.

The structure stood, however, in a desirable bedroom community north of Boston. It was renovated into a three-bedroom home.

Dropped ceilings are among the architectural features that help define spaces in what was once an abandoned barn. Barn remodeling allows unusual architecture features both outside and inside. The country kitchen is a highlight.

The stairs, as in most barns, are dramatic.

Note the cupola and weather vane.

93

Carriage House

This carriage house, once used to stable horses and as a garage, was part of an estate in Massachusetts. The client moved the structure and the caretaker's cottage down the road and planned to renovate them into a residence.

The remodeling process posed design challenges for the architect, Gene Racek. The client wanted to retain the carriage house effect, while eliminating any reminders of the interior's former use as a garage.

The old carriage house is now transformed. It makes a lovely, sprawling residence.

The living room windows bring in abundant light.

New construction was kept at a minimum since the client wanted to use the existing space. Racek's design added stairs to the outside and decks overlooking the fields.

Barn to Rental Home

Serena Watson, developer and designer, bought an old barn to convert into a rental home in a popular tourist area.

The top image shows the barn during the first few months of renovation. Note the transom over the sliding barn door. The town's historic commission didn't permit any major changes on the front of the barn. Inside, there was a good deal of work to be done. A lovely French door is now hidden behind that sliding barn door. The latter can be used, when privacy is desired. *Courtesy of D. Peter Lund.*

The upstairs area was turned into this beautiful balcony, which is a replica of the one in the local Congregational church. *Courtesy of D. Peter Lund.*

Above: A lovely weather vane graces the old cupola.

Below: A great deal of siding was done on the side of the barn, where new windows were also added. *Courtesy of D. Peter Lund.*

The exposed structural members add to the feeling of strength and dignity conveyed by the barn. *Courtesy of D. Peter Lund.*

97

Downstairs, there are well-lit guest or children bedrooms and extra living space. *Courtesy of D. Peter Lund.*

The barn is becoming beautiful again. *Courtesy of D. Peter Lund.*

The Onion Barn

The 28 by 40-foot barn was built on the North-South axis in the 1850s with a 16 by 28-foot shed addition to the North. The horse and cart stables were located under the barn as part of the foundation. The barren bleak land was the buffer zone between various groups of Native Americans.

The barn had undergone several minor conversions before the current owners hired Mark Farber to maintain its nature and building vocabulary and create a comfortable, all-season home that incorporated new functions, structures, rooms, and mechanical systems within its existing fabric in playful, inventive, and bold ways.

Farber faced many design challenges and restrictions. The existing timber frame challenged the introduction of four levels of living space and the staircases and landings to access them. There were very few undersized windows in the existing barn conversion and no outdoor living space adjacent to the primary living spaces. The stone foundation had originally been built "on grade" without concrete footings or mortar; the first floor framing sat on dirt. The timber frame second floor structure did not allow for the introduction of plumbing or wiring, and the original barn had been built 5 inches out of square.

Construction began with a period of deconstruction where the previous renovations were peeled back to reveal the bones of the barn. Windows were enlarged to meet code-mandated egress requirements and increase natural lighting within the dark barn. Square-punched windows were added at appropriate locations to provide additional lighting, ventilation, and views. The stables became boat storage and mechanical space and opened up, once again, with carriage doors to the lower pasture area. *Courtesy of D. Peter Lund.*

The barn remained a singular volume upon which later additions were made in the form of a shed addition and dormers, cupola, hipped-roof porch, wood deck, stone steps, and outdoor shower. Rough-sawn Atlantic White Cedar was used for the beveled clapboard siding and trim. Known for its qualities in boat building, the cedar was left to weather naturally. *Courtesy of Paul Doherty.*

The barn and shed addition wrap around the new wooden deck, creating the feeling that the deck is a true extension of the interior living space – an outdoor room. The deck with its built-in benches (no railings) steps down to the garden and to additional exterior living space where none existed before. *Courtesy of D. Peter Lund.*

Granite steps welcome guests at the public front entry. The doorknocker dates from 1834.
Courtesy of D. Peter Lund.

101

The stone-veneered foundation becomes stone retaining walls that extend out into the landscape to define outdoor living areas. The stones used came from the original foundation. *Courtesy of D. Peter Lund.*

From many vantage points and different levels, the visitor is repeatedly re-oriented back to the great room and its sandblasted stone and antique brick fireplace and chimney. The staircase and balcony railings are treated as a sculptural element that connects all four levels of the house, as the stairs make their way continuously up to the cupola. *Courtesy of Paul Doherty.*

The interior vistas were expanded to give the house a larger feel while maintaining a cozy human scale in each room. In the living room, the ceiling height soars to 27 feet up to the cupola. *Courtesy of Paul Doherty.*

Existing materials were often left in a rough, natural state to emphasize their tactile qualities. *Courtesy of D. Peter Lund.*

All rooms on all levels open directly to the great room. *Courtesy of D. Peter Lund.*

Through removing an exterior wall, Farber could incorporate the screened porch into the house as a sunroom facing due south. *Courtesy of D. Peter Lund.*

The kitchen was designed to be an inviting, flow-through space. Local cabinet-makers made the red birch cabinets, detailing them to look like pieces of free-standing furniture.

Courtesy of D. Peter Lund.

The island contains an oversized sink, which can be used from both sides. Fold down cutting boards expand the kitchen work surfaces when necessary. *Courtesy of D. Peter Lund.*

The second floor has two bedrooms, a bathroom, and a balcony/loft sitting area overlooking the fireplace below. The third floor has the master bedroom suite. *Courtesy of D. Peter Lund.*

The cupola with its motor-operated awning windows was introduced to reinforce the "barn" theme, as well as to provide natural lighting, ventilation, and a place to escape and view the ocean.

Courtesy of D. Peter Lund.

The standing seam barn roof is constructed from natural-weathering zinc, which is expected to have a 100-year lifespan. It reminds one of traditional metal-roofed barns. *Courtesy of D. Peter Lund.*

The plumbing is contained in this sculptural tree.

Courtesy of D. Peter Lund.

Green and Sustainable Design

Cho Benn Holback + Associates salvaged an historic barn and rebuilt it into a new studio residence while incorporating green and sustainable design principles and alternative energy sources. The firm designed a self-sustained energy system using passive solar, active solar, photo voltaic, dry composting waste, and gray water systems. The building utilized many sustainable building materials in the construction as well as concepts of perma-cultural living cycles. The unique character of the old stable and the milking stalls were preserved as features in the dwelling. The project focused on maintaining the integrity of the original stone foundation, wood structure, and interior details while converting this structure into a house and small animal shed.

South elevation after conversion with native drought-resistant wildflowers in the foreground. Water from the gray water system provides irrigation while the composting toilet waste provides fertilizer. *Courtesy of George Holback.*

The original South façade has limited windows and minimal access to views. The exterior siding was wood board and batten that was covered with a high content lead paint. The original roof was asphalt shingle. *Courtesy of George Holback.*

The original North entry façade had an asphalt driveway. Its siding and roof were identical in appearance and construction to the South side.

This close up of the South elevation shows the new fireplace made with gathered fieldstone. It also shows how the solar technologies on the roof are well hidden, thus not detracting from the historic character of the barn. *Courtesy of George Holback.*

The North side now shows the new grass paved driveway that was a green replacement for the original asphalt drive. It also shows the new metal roof made from partially recycled metal and the new roof ventilation system for natural ventilation and passive cooling. *Courtesy of George Holback.*

The stone wall beyond the animals was re-pointed and became a feature in the dining room. *Courtesy of George Holback.*

The original barn upper level was transformed into the main living room. *Courtesy of George Holback.*

Left: The original barn utilized an earthen ramp with parallel logs and a canvas covering for livestock access from the level above to the stalls below. This image shows the different levels. *Courtesy of George Holback.*

Right: The image shows the original side shed stalls that were later to become the bedroom area. *Courtesy of George Holback.*

The dining room adjacent to the kitchen is a dramatic transformation of the animal stalls and dirt floor. The new window and door opening to the South provide passive solar heating of the radiant floor slab as well as spectacular views to the valley and meadow below. The full array of solar heating systems is hidden behind the salvaged stall doors to the right. *Courtesy of George Holback.*

In the new living area, the entire ground floor area was also opened up with new doors. *Courtesy of George Holback.*

A Barn as a Connector

The owner of two 1860s log dwellings in Rushford, Minnesota, wanted a connecting annex. Mark Johnson of Terrasol Restoration & Renovation suggested placing a 1860s barn from Caledonia, Minnesota, between them, doubling the living area. The resulting new space blends seamlessly with the old.

The hand-hewn beams and supports from the original barn create an ambiance of pioneer authenticity while providing definition for the living and dining areas. *Courtesy of Terrasol Restoration and Renovation Company.*

The barn, originally from near New Prague, Minnesota, passed through several owners before it was dismantled and poorly sheltered in northern Minnesota. By the time Terrasol Renovation & Restoration was called on to erect a dwelling from the materials, the logs had begun to deteriorate. Replacement timbers from another barn of the same vintage were found to substitute for the ruined logs. The windows were salvaged from a local foundry. With the exception of the first floor framing, the entire project was accomplished with salvaged wood products. *Courtesy of Terrasol Restoration and Renovation Company.*

The kitchen enjoys natural light most of the day from an expanse of windows on the east wall and the clerestory above.

Courtesy of Terrasol Restoration and Renovation Company.

The original full loft was cut down to a half loft, creating a vaulted ceiling over the living space. The loft is the cabin's sleeping area. Because the loft joists were deteriorated, they were replaced with 3 by 12 inch joists from a 1870s flourmill in Sleepy Eye, Minnesota. *Courtesy of Terrasol Restoration and Renovation Company.*

Salvaged Sheds

For purely functional buildings, sheds *can* have interesting lives. Terrasol Restoration custom tailored this one to meet the needs of this century.

Many sheds start out deteriorated, dilapidated, and downright hopeless looking. *Courtesy of Terrasol Restoration and Renovation Company.*

The new stairs. *Courtesy of Terrasol Restoration and Renovation Company.*

A comfortable great room. *Courtesy of Terrasol Restoration and Renovation Company.*

Terrasol brings them back to life. *Courtesy of Terrasol Restoration and Renovation Company.*

Converted Granary

This timber frame home is a converted granary originally erected twenty miles from the present site. Terrasol changed its future through its renovation.

Transforming the granary with its telephone pole foundation and 30-foot beams saved it from the bulldozer. The house is partially earth sheltered on the slide of a slope. The two dormers were later additions to provide room for a walk-in closet and a separate bathroom for the master bedroom in the loft area. *Courtesy of Terrasol Restoration and Renovation Company.*

Terrasol worked with the owners to dismantle, move, restore, and rebuild it. Conventional siding sheaths the timber frame structure. *Courtesy of Terrasol Restoration and Renovation Company.*

Elm logs harvested from the property form the stairs. The second floor joists of the former granary were used to make the 2- by 12-inch treads. A stained glass star created by Terrasol and an angled window highlight the stairwell, where original timbers dramatically frame antique family photos. *Courtesy of Terrasol Restoration and Renovation Company.*

The original timbers have been left exposed in the kitchen and living areas, providing display shelving for antique carpentry tools and a collection of antique bottles and jars. The massive fieldstone fireplace provides supplemental heat to ward off Minnesota's infamous cold. *Courtesy of Terrasol Restoration and Renovation Company.*

The passive solar house is modeled after a New England saltbox. It is nestled into a south-facing hillside for maximum sun exposure. Many salvaged and recycled products have been used throughout. *Courtesy of Terrasol Restoration and Renovation Company.*

115

The master suite in the new link is full of light through the placement of skylights at the end walls and the windows mirroring each other on opposite walls. The ceiling reflects the roof lines of the new link. *Courtesy of Nick Wheeler Photography.*

Shaker Revision

The Beaver Valley Mills Barn is a restoration of a barn in Pennsylvania's Shaker country. The building was originally used for beaver pelt dyeing. The renovation was a complete gut of the interior and the re-cladding of the back second floor addition, along with a porch addition on the first floor.

Rupinder Singh/Mimar Design and Dan Martell were responsible for the architecture/design of the project; Dan Martell was both the owner and the contractor.

The mill peers out from between the summer foliage, a pristine structure on a modest hill. The junction between old and new construction is clearly delineated, yet abstracted by distance. *Courtesy of Rupinder Singh.*

A new porch is added to the kitchen on the ground floor, along with a substantial reworking of the windows/doors to integrate the new addition onto the original mill building. The scale of the porch overhang, the crisp edge of the roof rake, and the proportional relationship of solid walls to punched windows were key considerations in the renovation. *Courtesy of Dan Martell.*

How to create a wall that would wake one up in the morning yet keep one up at night? That was the challenge for the arched brick wall and fireplace. The prescription called for wagon wheels, barn pavers, and Shaker-like restraint. *Courtesy of Dan Martell.*

Windows are inherently moments in 22-inch thick walls. Salvaged shutters and tinted concrete sills ease the massive returns, along with angled jambs to extend light into the rooms. Yellow pine planks salvaged from an 1860 log cabin in Elizabethtown, Pennsylvania, serve as an honest floor. The planks are attached with cast iron nails for a truly vintage look. The stair treads are notched for the swing of the door. *Courtesy of Dan Martell.*

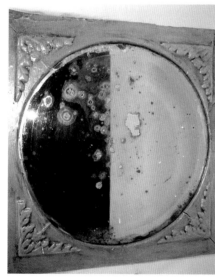

The master bathroom vanity is a rejuvenated dry sink with a yellow limestone top, glass tile backsplash, and a salvaged drawer chest. An antique mirror and flanking hand-blown glass pendant lights complete the image. *Courtesy of Dan Martell.*

Top: The shower is a three-dimensional tartan-like grid of white marble and colored glass tile accent banding. *Courtesy of Dan Martell.*

Center: Details. *Courtesy of Dan Martell.*

Bottom: Stairs. *Courtesy of Dan Martell.*

New York Barn

A traveling band of English barn builders built this barn in the late nineteenth century. Until it was purchased in 1991, it has been consistently used for hay and equipment storage.

Initially, the owners planned to use it for a bed and breakfast and hired Frank Falino, Architect. When it was completed, they were too fond of Falino's design to invite total strangers for overnight stays.

The barn is surrounded by central New York dairy farms. The intent for the exterior design was to maintain the simple barn form, line, and detailing. In the interior, Falino used post and beam techniques to complement, aesthetically as well as structurally, the original.

Two stone additions house the kitchen on the right end and the hearthroom on the left of the building. Here, we see the kitchen end.

The new siding system allows original siding inside the finish walls. *Copyright © 2003 Tim Wilkes 585.423.1966.*

The exterior siding, new stone veneer, and site-built furnishings all employ locally milled materials or those found inside the structure, or on the property.
Copyright © 2003 Tim Wilkes 585.423.1966.

From the dining room, you can see into the atrium. The original stone foundation walls are exposed. *Copyright © 2003 Tim Wilkes 585.423.1966.*

The atrium space with the kitchen in the background. There are rolled concrete floors, radiant heat, glass block pavers in ceiling (the floor of the attic), and old beams supported by new. *Copyright © 2003 Tim Wilkes 585.423.1966.*

And a warm, roaring hearth. *Copyright ©
2003 Tim Wilkes 585.423.1966.*

The table is made from "scraps," including the log beam for
the base. *Copyright © 2003 Tim Wilkes 585.423.1966.*

The view to the front entry. The bar and entertainment area is to the right. *Copyright © 2003 Tim Wilkes 585.423.1966.*

Chapter Five

COMMERCIAL & OTHER CONVERSIONS

Many villages and towns have old mills and barns that are slowly sliding into decay. In earlier decades, however, they may have been important landmarks.

Barns catch our attention. Perhaps they remind us of more romantic times or the continuity of history. Maybe we find them soothing antidotes to the pace of modern life or perhaps they remind us of the gentle cycles of nature.

Some creative developers and designers are willing to take up the challenge of reworking our architectural heritage to fit the resources and needs of the present. They see the potential that lies dormant in these old barns and have the energy and enthusiasm to bring it to light.

Adaptive Re-Use/Remodel

From the beginning, the mill has been a landmark for the village of Hebron (Ohio) and the surrounding area. Originally built at a significant crossroads in Ohio in the 1880s, the site overlooks the junction of the former Ohio Canal basin and the National Road (St. Rt. 40). The building served as a grain mill until the 1980s when it was abandoned.

In 2000, Brezina Design and Construction Services adapted the building to meet the needs of an architectural and construction firm. Their goal was to maintain as much of the building's integrity and historical value as possible.

Current building code requirements would not allow for use of the upper floors so the second floor had to be restored and turned into a mezzanine to enable partial use. This step provided openness in the building. Materials on site were used to patch holes, make doors, and finish the inside of the building. Old grain wheels were used as bases for glass top tables, and old doors were turned into countertops for the bathrooms.

To allow for required entrances/exits, the main drive-through area where trucks used to come through to drop off their loads was made into the entry and lobby. A ramp flows up from the back door where employees start their day. Thick, heavy doors greet clients at the front and back. The large canopy that protected the original entry was closed in with glass and made into the conference area for the design firm. The light that pours from this room at night welcomes passersby to the village.

Brezina bought the Mill in 1999. Notice the corrugated metal siding that was removed during the renovation of the building.

132

The front elevation today as it sits facing south on state route 40. *Courtesy of Suzanne Sullivan of Brezina Design Services.*

The major challenge of the project was integrating the new with old for the purpose of designing an environment where creativity is a way of life. The contrasts are obvious. Curving track lighting and pendent lights hang from solid wood beams. Grain shoots and old milling equipment are adjacent to computers and drafting tables. A curved wall greets clients as they look up through the original beams to the third floor.

Above: Close up of the front doors to the right and the conference room with the large canopy over the glass enclosed room. *Courtesy of Suzanne Sullivan of Brezina Design Services.*

Below: Looking up the ramp from the back door towards the front doors and waiting area. The spindles on the railing were purchased at an auction. *Courtesy of Suzanne Sullivan of Brezina Design Services.*

Above: Looking up the brick walk to the back entrance to the office. *Courtesy of Suzanne Sullivan of Brezina Design Services.*

Below: The conference room is located where the old front door used to be under the large outside canopy. The doors slide on tracks like barn doors. A triangle cut out refers to the Brezina Design and Construction logo. The base of the glass top table is an old grain mill wheel; another large wheel can be seen on the wall. *Courtesy of Suzanne Sullivan of Brezina Design Services.*

The ambiance is exquisite.
Courtesy of D. Peter Lund.

Private nooks for quiet conversations or reflections about a more relaxed life are scattered here and there under the barn's soaring, 30-foot ceiling.

Courtesy of D. Peter Lund.

All this elegance in what was once a cattle barn. *Courtesy of D. Peter Lund.*

Sustainable Green Preservation

The Westmoreland Conservation District, Pennsylvania, was founded in 1949 to help farmers practice good stewardship of their soil, streams, and forests. In later decades, as times and the economy changed, the District extended its educational stewardship efforts to include others who work regularly with the area's natural resources such as developers, loggers, and earthmovers. In the late 1990s, it expanded those efforts to include the general public.

The cornerstone of this effort was a new Conservation Education Center. A 120-year-old barn was donated to the Westmoreland Conservation District. The barn was disassembled and carefully transported fifteen miles from its original location.

The primary goal of the client was to design a space that reflected the conservation philosophy of the district.

The proposed building would complement the environment, be energy efficient, and use indigenous materials and local craftsmen for its execution. The final project features a gray water reclamation system, geothermal radiant floor heating, and natural light and ventilation. Strategic building location and plant selection maximize the benefits of the local climate and ecosystem.

The building's careful siting, for instance, makes maximum advantage of the sun's warmth in the winter and the prevailing breezes in the summer, reducing dependence on mechanical systems for these necessities. Elongating the structure's East-West axis allows the Center to draw significant natural warmth from the southern sun. In summer, a canopy to reduce heat gain shades south-facing windows. Surrounding native landscaping adds beauty while conserving water use.

After nearly 120 years of agricultural service, a 7,600 square foot bank barn stood in the direct path of a new housing development. A community effort saved it from demolition and transformed it into the keystone of a new conservation education campus in southwestern Pennsylvania. *Courtesy of Justin Merriman.*

Amish craftsmen spent months carefully dismantling the original 1880s-era barn, marking each of the more than three hundred hand-hewn beams and timbers with a code so they could be rejoined in exactly the same way when the building was reconstructed at its new location a few miles away. *Courtesy of Justin Merriman.*

In adapting the barn for its new use as an Education Center, the District and Pittsburgh architect, A. Richard Glance, worked to incorporate recycled/recyclable materials, energy-efficient fixtures, and a variety of low-maintenance, sustainable technologies so that the structure itself would be a teaching tool: a working model of conservation in action. *Courtesy of Justin Merriman.*

The barn has a 25-foot peak and a massive frame of 6- to 10-inch thick oak and poplar timbers. Examples of conservation are built into the inside of the structure. The concrete floor of the main meeting room, for instance, provides thermal mass and helps in passive solar performance. *Courtesy of Justin Merriman.*

The Center's main meeting room allows it to be comfortably adapted for use by a variety of different-sized groups. *Courtesy of Justin Merriman.*

The interior walls of the Center feature chestnut boards original to the barn, freshly planed to reveal their beauty. Recently harvested low-grade cherry, poplar, ash, and maple also have been used to finish the interior walls. Yellow poplar, sawed on site, was used as siding for the Center's new exterior. *Courtesy of Justin Merriman.*

The offices of the Westmoreland Conservation District staff are located where the grain, animals, and farm equipment were housed. *Courtesy of Justin Merriman.*

Reclaiming a barn about to be lost to development is practicing the conservation ethic that the building's owner, the Westmoreland Conservation District, preaches. More than 80% of the barn's original timbers of poplar, white oak, red oak, and chestnut were reused. They actually are in such fine shape that they should be able to stand and serve in their new purpose for at least another 120 years. *Courtesy of Justin Merriman.*

The 7,600 square foot center is a working model of conversation in action. In addition to its energy-efficient design, the project demonstrates the deconstruction and conversion of a building and the use of iron oxide from acid mine drainage for finishes. *Courtesy of Justin Merriman.*

Below: The Education Center models conservation. The Center's shell is made of structural insulated panels produced locally. They are a "sandwich" of waste wood with non-CFC-producing foam in between. The stone foundation is recycled from another nearby barn. The floor of the two rear decks is covered with a protective coating made entirely of recycled automobile tires from Pennsylvania. All windows are low-E to control thermal radiation. *Courtesy of Justin Merriman.*

Pine Haven Cemetery Barn

KBA Architects designed the complete restoration of the Pine Haven Cemetery Barn and 1880s barn on the site of the Seminatore family farm. The site was originally the location of Burlington's poor farm, where people traveling through town could set up temporary shelters while they established themselves locally or moved on to other localities. Over time, the property was deeded to the town of Burlington, Massachusetts, for the establishment of the Pine Haven Cemetery intended for residents of Burlington or family members of town residents.

Existing wood framing required shoring over the years to repair dry rot and insect infestation. *Courtesy of Knight, Bagge & Anderson, Inc.*

The image shows the pre-renovation post and beam construction with the hayloft above. *Courtesy of Knight, Bagge & Anderson, Inc.*

The barn had fallen into considerable disrepair. If the actions of the committee and town had not saved the structure, it would have been condemned and demolished. *Courtesy of Knight, Bagge & Anderson, Inc.*

After the complete restoration of the exterior and interior, the new main entrance to the Pine Haven Cemetery Barn and chapel does not resemble that of a barn. *Courtesy of Knight, Bagge & Anderson, Inc.*

New rear elevation with the large stained glass chapel window faces the grounds. *Courtesy of Knight, Bagge & Anderson, Inc.*

Entrance into new non-denominational chapel has a 14-foot stained glass wall depicting a waterfall in an untouched landscape setting. *Courtesy of Knight, Bagge & Anderson, Inc.*

The renovated chapel is used for funeral services.

Courtesy of Knight, Bagge & Anderson, Inc.

New entrance hall accesses cemetery offices and the chapel.

Courtesy of Knight, Bagge & Anderson, Inc.

The Brickyard Barn Inn

The Brickyard Barn Inn is a 1927 dairy barn with a unique red brick exterior and attached silo. In 1926, Kansas State architecture students designed the barn, which was built with $5,000 by William Baird, who was almost bankrupted by the cost. The dairy consisted of attached silo, milking stalls for thirty-six cows, and two bullpens. The large red glazed brick on the building exterior is considered unusual and was probably very expensive.

The barn survived the 1951 Topeka flood. In 1954, Baird auctioned off his dairy assets, but it is said that at least one cow was housed in the barn until around 1963.

In 1974, the Baird family sold the barn and about four acres to Mr. and Mrs. Robert Straub, who remodeled the huge hayloft into a three-bedroom home and began the removal of iron stalls and concrete with the intention of creating an antique store. During the next eighteen years, various families purchased the "home" and added to the property. In 1993, one family opened a bed and breakfast, calling it the Brickyard Barn Inn.

Today, the Inn is used for weddings, dinners, destination weekends, and advertising location shots, including newspaper special events sections.

Left: A visitor can lounge on the deck while watching a beautiful sunset across the fields of corn.

Bottom left: Breakfast is served on the main floor of the converted dairy barn. A country kitchen, formal dining room, and an elegant living room with fireplace complete the facility.

Bottom right: Casual country charms marks this attractive spot.

Today, the 1927 dairy barn has become a popular B&B
and wedding reception location in Topeka, Kansas.

The clients are happy with their barn. Their two kids roller-blade on the concrete slab and can literally climb the walls. The structure gives them the space they desire, and the cost of the entire 4,800 square foot house was kept under $200,000.

A nice finishing touch is located outside in a pine grove. The clients took an old industrial tumbler for leather tanning, tilted it on end, cut a hole in the side for a door and put in a wood-burning stove. On cold winter nights the entire clan can be found in the sauna, very content. *Courtesy of Greg Premru.*

Chapter Seven

WADSWORTH VILLAGE

Recycling old barns allows new needs to be met with a minimum of disruption to a community and is often more marketable than new construction.

The reuse of old buildings physically links us to our past. They have become a part of our cultural heritage, and their preservation helps to anchor us in an increasingly diverse society. The rehabilitation of old barns preserves their unique architectural beauty and retains the character and scale they add to the environment.

New England's charms lie in its past and present: in its rocky fields and forested hiking trails, in the Boston Pops and high technology, in revolutionary war taverns and cozy country inns.

Previously known as Salem Village, Danvers, Massachusetts, was made a township in 1757. During the 1760s and 1770s, Danvers took a politically active role in the growing revolutionary turmoil; seven Danvers minutemen were killed in the first armed struggle during the Lexington Alarm of April 19, 1775. During the Revolution, Danversport became a prominent shipping and shipbuilding center. The nineteenth century saw Danvers growing industrially and culturally.

Today, Danvers, Massachusetts, recognizes its heritage through annual celebrations and an office park that contains a nineteenth century school, a church, seven houses, and several barns. Unlike many of today's developers, one developer and architect took some of the local heritage and reshaped it into office space for the future.

Danvers was a farming community with onion farms and dairies. When Interstate 95 was built, the area was dramatically changed.

Wadsworth Village was the dream of entrepreneur Fred Schaeffer and his wife Carol. He wanted to create an "incubator park" for fledgling business. Then, they attended a lecture on the beginnings of Old Sturbridge Village, which preserves history in time.

In 1982, Schaefer bought the former Wadsworth elementary school building and 2.6-acre lot from the town of Danvers. He promised to renovate it in keeping with its nineteenth century flavor and to rent it out at low cost to small start-up companies. He converted the classrooms to office space and preserved the exterior of the c. 1897 schoolhouse.

Seizing on the market opportunity, Schaefer decided to find as many antique buildings as possible, within the local area, site them as in a village, and renovate them into office space.

Schaefer, Boston architect Gene Racek, of E.R. Racek Associates, and landscape architect John Wacker of Weston, Massachusetts, drew up plans for Wadsworth Village in Danvers. Racek designed the site plan for the village with the village green.

He and Schaefer sought out and moved historic houses and barns, many slated for demolition, into the area. These were moved to the site, where they were situated around the common area. The wishes of the new tenants drove the design of the interior office spaces.

Ultimately, the village contains a broad selection of office space for growing companies, ranging from single offices to 5,500-square feet of multi-use space in nineteenth century farmhouses or barns. The village was designed to serve growing companies, to maximize productivity, conserve time, and minimize expenses.

The model village.

Details.

Turn-of-the-century houses and barns were moved and renovated into office buildings, giving them new life.

The work involved the dismantling, relocating, reconstructing, and converting of historic buildings.

Today, the village is a charming alternative to an office park.

Some of the buildings were transported long distances.

The sliding barn doors have become a lovely French door.